A MADDER GHOST

MARTYN CRUCEFIX

A Madder Ghost

London
ENITHARMON PRESS
1997

First published in 1997
by the Enitharmon Press
36 St George's Avenue
London N7 0HD

Distributed in the UK and Europe
by Password (Books) Ltd.
23 New Mount Street
Manchester, M4 4DE

Distributed in the USA and Canada
by Dufour Editions Inc.
PO Box 7, Chester Springs
PA 19425, USA

© Martyn Crucefix 1997

ISBN 1 900564 10 6

Typeset in 10pt Bembo by Bryan Williamson, Frome,
and printed in Great Britain by
The Cromwell Press, Broughton Gifford, Wiltshire

Contents

Ante
The fugitive / 9
Causeway / 10
After Rumi / 11
Trojan women / 12
Sighting / 13
These strangers / 14
A bird's edge / 15
Childhood / 16
Under Highgate / 17
The thumb-print / 18
Shrinking back / 19
Commonest of things / 20
Till darkness clears / 21
Pietà / 22

Belly Pains on Princelet Street / 25

Post
Yellow Pages / 59
Lips / 60
A documentary / 61
Footprint / 62
A try-out / 63
Nightmare / 64
La-la-la / 65
The gift / 66
Loneliness / 67
Recognition / 68
Skin / 69
A tiny prison / 70
Something we did / 71
New lullaby / 72
Head tale / 73

Restless child   /   74
Empty the bath   /   75
The short light   /   76
You wave   /   77
Hold me   /   78
Kyrie   /   79

ANTE

Note: The first and third sections of this book are dedicated to my son Thomas. The ante-natal condition referred to in the poem 'Childhood' is sometimes associated with birth defects. This led my wife and me to agree to an amniocentesis test which – after we'd spent several weeks anxiously weighing up how we might respond to bad news – reassured us, thankfully, that there was no serious problem.

The fugitive

Its biggest moment,
this re-make of television,
where Harrison Ford flings himself
from his pursuers,
from the white, half-moon of a dam,
his rag-body rotating slowly,
falling with water into water

too far to be true
so there's the feel of the infinite
in it and at the least
you know he will be altered

– this, before a meal with parents
where we've resolved not to say
what we immediately say

how that morning you were late
and dabbling in the bathroom
with tiny chemistry
from which you read your body,
discovered the broken limit
of the thin blue line
that rose towards the window

and how we laughed then
and eating later, again laughed,
hardly knowing what to feel

though steadied by your mother
who was wanting us to recommend,
or not, our choice of film.

Causeway

(Holy Island)

How sick you were with it,
one foot over the threshold,
enough, the sight of the roof,
the way the kitchen's wood stove
stank up the rented cottage
so absolutely
as to involve itself
in every hormonal flood-tide
bled through you those weeks

– how it would not let go

even stiffening to watch a fox
slip into the high dunes
of Holy Island, the memory
of it still overwhelming
the tide-covered causeway,
the ripped-off edge of waves
beating on Bamburgh Castle

where you turned to the camera
with such delight in your eyes,
hair all over the place,
entwined as the Gospels' lines,
their self-pleasing spiritual,
the hooked beaks of birds
steadying themselves to dive
into the stink of sea,
the uncertain physicality
of blood and quick and well-being.

After Rumi

These, the fruit of efforts
to be *crumbled*
as Rumi writes in a fragment
someone showed me
and I scribbled down and now

it has struck up
over this real creativity
we've stirred between us

and these few lines I want
to hold in apprehension,
not dissect, to contain
and connect
the way things are, since
so little grows on jagged rock

(this is what Rumi says)

so be ground, be crumbled
so that wildflowers
will come up where you are.

Trojan women
(Barbican, London)

Your mother's taken on an awful
role as a Trojan woman

and the familiar, heroic years
of war seem longer already
than they did before,
each moment now another drop
in the brew of influence
we concoct for you

adrift beneath her diaphragm,
thumping like a neighbour
overhead, as she sings
and comes to understand
the women as they emptied
onto Scamander Plain
to find the Greek invader gone

and finding the horse
and pulling it home,
pulled through the walls of home
to shattered household gods,
fruitless libations

of every woman fleeing, amazed
at what she helped bring in,
her husband silent on the ground,
soul whistling at the riverside.

Sighting

Money in a machine
for a picture of the occasion

and once inside, your shirt up,
waistband down,
cold jelly smeared over
and a night-scene breaks open
to night-sky, uncertainty,
inner space and fluid stars

a black angle
of shimmering topography,
looming up and withering off
as the mike is pressed home
in a bizarre interview
with our unborn's bulbous head

– gritty, tiny floods and streams
of arms, legs, a pearl string
of stepping stones
for a back
and this – I remember thinking –
is a biology lesson, my squinting
down the barrel
of a microscope,
clumsy, focussing through layers
and tubes and vessels,
anxious for some detail
I'd overshot, racked back to

as the nurse is doing right now

as if she's alighted on something
more than interesting
and says, *Fine, that's just fine –
I'll call a doctor to explain,*
and she leads us out to wait
with our picture, a black leaf.

These strangers

We do not have it yet,
but we two are the real bad news
to be put back
like broken toys into a room
with the other first-glimpsers

the first-portraits-
of-our-fruitfulness,
the oh-what-perfect-tiny-hands,
delighters in a snub-nose,
the eye-pit lookers-on

– now, we are the grotesques

flimsy as cartoons, folding ourselves
into bolted chairs, each
stricken with a molten storm
overhead, monstrous,
specific and as fearful
of scaring these strangers
as of the news we do not have

since they have already
glimpsed it, begun to guess
why we do not move off
as we should and their looks
accuse us, say we have betrayed
every last imagined, petted ounce.

A bird's edge

Rage, sickness, slithering,
though both still sat tight,
flung back on ourselves,
our sole selves this time,
not even that years-familiar
lean-to of each other

(one strong, one weak,
one weak, one strong enough)

but that solitary inadequate
who walks right through
what we thought we were
in moments like this
(though what else like this?)
the bleating creature
who'd have the world halt

– that, the sharpest sensation

a bird's edge through air,
the scald of its passing,
the irrevocable wind
that wearies us down
and will wear us out quite,
that has settled in our hearts
and with it come suffering

and what it is that we sow,
whether this three months return
or some life-long exchange

we take the consequences.

Childhood

The god-like avuncular,
the feelingly-scientific,
a little mother, a little father

though it's not her child
who presents bilateral cysts
in its foetal brain
like a pair of spectacles
perched at the back of its head

– nor does she see them
as we do, the ghost-trace
of our own incredulous gaze,
the gape of big zeroes
in our first child's impression,
first screen appearance
which she's marked down already
as a problem in prospect

perhaps a neural childhood
in a body that will outlive us

and she explains in a tone
she's trained for the job,
asks once, twice, *you understand?*

Under Highgate

On the pavement, at the foot
of Highgate's long hill,
a man and a woman walk together
and want to be deaf
to the sliver of dissension
that has stiffened their tongues
since they slowly came
from the Whittington
and now steadily up the hill

in such silence as falls
behind speech that has wound
its way from the glad day
to utter darkness and set it
trembling, a frantic noise
hardly to be answered
by a couple such as this

their genteel surroundings

such – of course – a perfect day
of children in strollers,
the café's red paint gleaming,
buses late, on time, not at all.

The thumb-print

Something like two dark rivers
wind down the hillside
from the red-painted café
to the whitened rooms again

the high table they lay you out on

like water, trembling
to the black core and naked,
unpeeled on the display
where the needle's plunged to draw
the urinous, wheat-coloured,
crumb-flecked fluid

the thumb-print of our child
we have given permission
to be taken, though it will
take them weeks to read it

and afterwards, we are finished,
since at some point we talked
till there's nothing to be said

ringing friends only to cancel,
for TV all afternoon,
evening, all night if we could.

Shrinking back

For weeks I fail you, failing
to see you as I once did

alert, alive, some growing
son or daughter – instead
fall to paltry self-defence,
from instinct maybe
but no less guilty for that

since this unwilled abortion
of a possibly imperfect thing's
a luxury, the kind of denial
closed to a mother who has slid
her hand into a pocket

found another's hand there,
small, unlearned and shrinking
back slowly as a sigh.

Commonest of things

Something of art, the slyness
of it, it occurs to me now,
since I cannot recover
the least detail of the moment
you sprung back into being

as if it happened out of frame
or I've scrapped every path
that could lead to the place
where such memories sink
their special profundity,
some self-protecting file
that has now enriched itself
with the all-but biblical return
you never gave up on

– repaid our uncertainties
with singlemindedness,
not one moment's doubt
of the witless machinery
that drove you into creation

or the phone-call (was that it?)

that would set us free
for the commonest of things,
to imagine your arrival,
to sit long over instant coffee
with colour charts for a room,
while you went right ahead,
happening furiously

readying for a conclusion,
O little redemption,
the rest of our lives.

Till darkness clears

(Derwentwater)

We've driven here for Easter's
withering and re-birth,
though the Spring we left
staking its claim in the south,
lags weeks behind

so we wake again to cold,
stare down at windowless streets
desolated by sleep,
become empty waiting ground

till darkness clears – then go,
bright, erect, up breezy trails
to the heights,
our child buried safe inside,
sleeping like clockwork
if you keep a steady tread

– but you're worn out,
content to let me cross alone,
to wander round Castlerigg's
corral of freezing stones,
its pattern of old worship,
some rite of celebration
you understand as I shiver
in the field, watch you turn,
flinch, all but stumble

as it starts awake, a smack
in your belly for being alive
and a perfect answer for life.

Pietà

We pack a radio to relax

– becomes a blithe soundtrack
over suffering,
stopped only by The News
that has us screaming at politics,
its greed and earthly powers
an irrelevance
to the *pietà* we will make
after hours of pain
and mystery and the dancing

keep upright, keep on the move

as if the pain's a blow-fly
we might chase to earth
and destroy once, for all

while I spray water to cool
and with each gasp
feel your temperature rise,
your body beginning
to gape like a bear trap,
all chains and razor teeth
and absence of control

as light freshens the window
showing it still going on,
so many days since last night
when I read Dick Francis
for the first time in my life,
waiting for contractions

and you sink with your back to me,
slung limp from my arms
like the impossibility of flight,
hair wet with the effort
and damp with my weeping
at the ghastly calculation
of this thing

where *pax, stop, enough, enough*
have no virtue at all,
only gas and air,
rasped by a diver
who is herself the sea,
out of which is drawn the core

a soaking-scalped purplish boy.

BELLY PAINS ON PRINCELET STREET

(for my father)

Note: In the 1680s, my Huguenot ancestors, clockmakers by profession, fled religious persecution by French officialdom and the military (the feared *dragonnades*) to settle in Spitalfields. In some of these poems, I have created, from their plight, an individual voice which progresses through infancy, eviction and flight to a new life as an immigrant in London, facing arson as well as abuse, to eventual marriage and return to France as a soldier. I have crossed this story with my own fears in my father's fight against illness because any understanding of it must, I believe, embrace the self-involvement of imagination.

Already closed, what I came here for,
why I'm at a loss, visiting window
after window, beyond Commercial Street.
This April afternoon's bolts
of blue sky unroll, extravagant,
above *Ganesa Sweets, New Balti, Raj,*

but I'm scared the pain in my belly
will sooner or later be history.
Walk away from it, to dusty windows
crammed with shoes, lean
my forehead at spasms like my father's.
Walk away from it, to the Mosque,

the Synagogue, what was once a Church
where immigrant mothers and fathers
came to pray out their exile, whose rootless
shadow I've become, coming for Rosa's
La Rochelle, finding her pictures
off the wall, the door I lean into, locked.

This is not something I've imagined.
It makes no sense to hear nothing
but myself, especially here,
the babble of voices on Fournier, Weaver
and Shuttle Street. In the filthy glass,
glare my father's eyes,

floating among shoes waiting to be filled.
It's nonsense in Dad's case.
It's real, frightening, so intimate,
almost reassuring to discover
we don't inherit their hair, eye-sight,
strong legs, lips, noses alone,

but also our parents' diseases.
Under the Mosque, the Synagogue, the Church,
I could find family bones that suffered
belly pains on Princelet Street
(bones, there are – and pain – but most, my voice –
of what there is, is anger)

One voice like another (by this
ghosted – that once, behind a poor curtain
where we had to wash after, once more, fires
on Weaver Street – this, at a bowl, spilled
that morning by someone slip-fingered –
so beneath the drape stood a flood

lost on a tiled floor, a white mirror –
till she glided, in a blanket, the curtain past
and on the ground – from long habit
of searching – of my eye – blocks of light
found silver, grey-black, unfolding
a reflection, her bending – naked to reach

her behind, twisting as to pray –
she reached forward, backwards, trembling
to wash – me standing, stirring, at love,
hardly knowing – going to know – and crowned,
at her breasts, astonished, at such riches
caught with eyes to the cold floor)

Passing workmen's boards sprayed B N P
BLACK CUNTS, loud, brittle radios
clashing with speakers in Weaver Street's
shop doorways as I walk home,
I realise I'm not breathing.
This must be the trickle-down of hurt.

In my jacket, a *La Rochelle* flier,
sketch of riverbank, mud, a moonlit body.
And the first I knew anything of it,
was Dad's own voice on the phone,
making light – cheery nothings for minutes,
sparing me, till a flash:

Saturday nights, the downward hill home,
three kids in the back and Dad slipping
to neutral for the long quiet flight,
that slowing-down suspense, the wait, the nudge
into gear, lurch, the motor's rise
and we would all breathe again.

(not at the table, there, but beneath –
sat I between my father's boots,
as he – a man of detail, he – touch,
delicacy, accurate to such a very little –
to his mechanisms and time, his joy – pounded
the King's head – that table

as if it were that head –
making shiver his tools and wheels and lenses –
whimpering, she, her sandalled feet – crying
peace, for it in household, country, me
now, at talk turned to *dragonnades* –
the repeating, that worship has ceased,

by order, of beatings, worse, rape –
lawless laws, God's absence, or seeming so,
and in the dark – in the dark,
imagined – a toddler, unknowing – I,
how they'd black-coated and marauding come
for us, each, to our beds – and I was true)

I phone a doctor friend for help.
'Tell me this. Has he been passing blood?'
(Would he ever tell me such a thing?)
'Maybe just piles. Or it might be much worse.
Haven't the doctors told him?'
A moment's pause, 'Hasn't he told you?'

And this is the way I do things.
Think through the worst, then hope
for something better. Yet I'm ashamed
at my own reaction: *Is this what's to come?*
My turning to look for blood in the pan?
I straighten up outside Durhani Brothers.

Under the left rib, a compression, sharp,
packed into shrinking space,
relieved a little with a straightened back.
Other days, the righthandside
and sometimes lying in bed, it bloats
to a pregnant swell I may not survive.

(jumped, at the roaring of him – I, stumbling
from bed to see the black-bearded captain
come to billet soldiers – but not upon all,
so careful this, at these houses only –
heretic, heretic –
and she weeping, my might-be brother in her,

to be birthing soon and they, playful,
striking at the fire – her fire,
the blackened hearthwork – the place of care,
meat, of talk – the fire sparked up –
and they, the captain, not guessing at us,
lifting skirts – legs white and dimpled

I saw, never before – and to roast
her leg-backs there, her fire, made by her
and would, some few times more make –
he, knife threatened for this – the billetting
of the *dragonnades* – screaming at the hearth –
at but the burn, did they cease)

(so orderly, once, our rooms –
the yellow arc pushed stenching now
into flames from the slit trouser-flap –
or tongue-hanging, the white creamy spittle
on my shoulder – and for food,
roared day long, twelve bellies – as quiet ached

our own, till thrown to the dogs, dish on dish,
once prepared – and she, spared much worse,
once the black-bearded, he had gone –
for her condition, used, as a fruit,
long bitten open, grown soft, unappetising –
was she to them (otherwise, not thought),

who had their fill elsewhere – by night
we heard – and all for faith –
our houses rather, then stamp out our faith –
the house-carcass, crawled armed idle flies on –
in leaving – so told me later, my father –
our return again home was most's hope)

I call on my brother. We cannot help ourselves.
We do not know what's wrong with him.
At traffic lights, I watch two workmen
in bright oilskins wash each other down
carefully, with a brush and hose,
unspeaking, intimate, cooperative,

the slurry collecting at their feet
(so proven, sentinel-poplars behind the house,
useless — black against the sky's
full star spread — then into the woods,
to the shadows — unfamiliar, he,
uncomfortable, straightening at some hurt —

we children crying only — at those greetings
made there — *Comrade, comrade* — useless)
But Dad holds out, inscrutable, cheerful.
I don't believe he's been told what it might be
and Mum is his weeping companion,
a catch in her throat over any small thing.

(nothing, of our words themselves — how
explained he our sufferings —
do I remember — but one word struck home
to us both — this with my brother,
Michael, did we times talk over and over —
blurring the real, the imaginary,

perhaps, but true as true is, ever —
and that of his telling, all could be boiled
away to that word, which
as he spoke it — Michael and I knew,
and we have spoken of this too,
also each to each —

knew we how — children, remember,
we were then — how the whole of God's realm
blighted must be and tearful —
as the rain that fell all over us all —
for never before, nor ever after,
spoke he the word — and speaking, cried)

Refugee. The networked voices,
the instant I'm through my front door.
That again, and *exile*.
By the time I'm ready to eat (skipping
garlic and onions might do some good),
armies agree to leave the mountain,

camps of the disappeared might be opened up.
But by the time I break up the company,
at Cleopatra's squalling –
Some innocents 'scape not the thunderbolt –
expelled out, under the sky-blocking
Barbican Towers,

certain my father is dying and I –
nor anybody else – can do a damned thing,
but want to beat up childish fists in the air
and roar out loud – want him to hear me
rage without an object. I do that.
I do that. I feel no better for it.

(to the woods had gone, before us,
the many thousands – to the waters then,
from La Rochelle – a trade in lives worth,
than betrayal to soldiers,
only a little less – long forest floors,
the tearing litter, feet, ill-shod – the trail,

of shadow-striped, sun-lipped vineyards,
their strands as wet hair combed
long across hillsides – lizards quickening
dusty rivulets into the grass –
dark, the dusty laurel – heat – and dark –
the cranking of midday bells, in hiding –

into moonlight, a clifftop, near midnight
and questions, angry, to the guide,
to challenge him who we had to trust –
but shrugged, he did – late, too late –
we had then no choice – saying,
but not into our own blood would he lead us)

It's done. Certain. It's started.
The words he would not speak, or have spoken.
Unwanted whispering . . . *Growth. Tumour*
(it was of moonlight, I remember –
remember, I say, though,
re-run, times, countless – rehearsed

till what was is a story,
what story was to a certainty –
yet, as this thumbnail of my right hand,
my knife hand, was the moon – and held up
to see it, was I – perhaps –
by God, to be seen – some small defiance,

perhaps that – a schooner,
its long boat flaking from the dark side –
its own reflection, chasing black waters across –
to a tiny cove – a whistle, sudden – hooves –
dragoons at charge – firing, from the shadows –
then broke we the miles wide beach across)

(our last words — as ever — *with us, be God*)
Waiting at Paddington for the home train,
I feel bloated, drum-tight, hungry
and the last thing I want
are these words urging at their own speed
(last words — yet by a dragoon,

on a galloping horse, shot — across the beach,
uneven, by the moon's unfaithful light,
one musket ball, to her, found its way —
and was he there — God —
gathering us to the boat, all —
for his great fatherhood, his temple —

yet one, from home running — for faith,
running, for him, for God —
one musket ball, to her, found its way —
and was he there — God —
into patriotic sand, she, face down, dead,
a life dying more slowly inside her —
and what does she, still, lying there, mother,
bearer, love, blood, teach?)

(of hatred, shows the wisdom –
of suffering, the fruitlessness of mercy –
of the stratagem of dogs, it holds good –
of threat given, answered must it be
by such force, immediate,
irretrievable, unrestrained,

as to offer, for a counter charge, no chance –
of suspicion, answer hatred –
of blow, make out an answer, three blows –
of circumstance, the worst
devise, anticipate –
of blood – blood spilt – how sacrosanct –

of pain, its long inheritance –
of God, his absence –
this all, in that moment, the ship
turning for England, I had not –
but anger, the unjust, love of family,
its seeds were in me)

Bolt upright to a mortar shell, in fact,
in the blackout of my old bedroom,
sighing with that much explosive power
from their room. Long drawn up,
trailing away moans, little pants in between,
her higher voice,

humming, anxious. All prior tensions
out in an instant, the probable devils,
though he seemed well as we walked
and – how could we? – not voiced a word
of what we knew grew inside.
Loose-kneed now, useless at their bedroom door,

the scene is doubled in the mirror.
She kneels on his righthandside of the bed.
He's crumpled, teeth out, jawless, greyed,
a halo from the pink bedside lamp.
Once, she tears her gaze from his to my face.
I go to make the tea.

(all we had then, clutching at them,
as floats – bundles only, wrapped and tied
by her who lay upon the sand –
moon-glints of fighting tackle in circle,
surrounding her, the dumb, down-looking soldiery –
and fled we, at full sail – I could not cry)

Back-arching in class, a slow squeeze
in my right side, awkward,
I walk across the room for relief.
Under these clouds, Dad is downing Picolax
for the doctors. Under these clouds,
a final purge for the knife – and Jessica,

beautiful and sassy as her namesake,
does my job, firing up the class on *The Merchant*,
whose 'do we not bleed' is no metaphor
for parents and grandparents
who start awake still to hammering doors,
cleared Quarters, old crammed sudden flight.

(to suburbs in the east, lapped
by tongues, familiar – of Lefevre, Roi, Duval –
in hundreds, weaver, shoemaker, gunsmith –
of Charlatt, Courtauld, Berbier, Maturin –
hairdresser, jeweller, and we, clockmakers,
bustled, homeless, making homes, at –

and growing – remember, the years old boy,
four, five, six – made out of inheritance,
clever, swift – by life, angry,
by such ill-timed hurt for school –
so beyond our streets, pricked, restless,
west and north, to words blurried,

focussing slowly – yet meaning
remembered, the tone out of other mouths –
in language felt still my old own,
enough to understand the spat *shit*, the *little cunt* –
Your Da got my job, the *Jew, Papist, Jew*,
the *fuck you whore*, the *fuck your mother*)

Snatches of old songs punctuate
his wide-eyed deliriums, mile-high
on anaesthetic dregs, painkillers, God-knows
from pale, watery drips, hung
about the bedstead, their measured
feeding of the bruised back of his hand

like old-fashioned water-clocks.
Others drain out the groin, penis,
the juice and waste of the cutting knife.
Restless, abroad, *Better to avoid
Bath city centre. He's a crook. Don't be long.*
In the white fist of his mask,

I see a riverbank, a brown boot-lace snake,
an outgrowth of the mud, its jaws
clamped to the snout of a red-finned fish.
Dragged, inched up the moonlit bank,
the fish lies still, gills gaping,
despairingly, flips itself like a coin.

(as calm as a clock, Michael, his heart,
it must be – toiling, learning it allows him,
apprentice maker of his own easy time –
while liquor, corroding books, at the loose ends
of my days – my baying out the ass
God, his sickness, humility, his compassions –

at eighteen, I was – my father, sixty-five –
for paring his widowerhood, the reasons of it –
he strikes me a blow – the pair of them,
at the magnifying lens – down it Michael stares,
yet who fires a neighbours' house, none sees –
charred jagged roof as the bitterness bred it

as anger in me, multiplying out –
as move in, they must – *comrade, comrade* –
and their daughter, behind the rigged, quick,
poor curtain – the cold morning
sharpening her breasts upon the tiled floor –
pleasing, appeased – love – somewhile)

A dark raspberry wound, stitched
like old pelt, or cloth, his skin glittering
at points with staples on his belly
to close a messy caesarean.
The drains have gone, one solitary drip
high on a portable stand

that he pushes to and fro around the bed
and beneath it all, himself,
come back from wherever the drugs,
the vicious persecution of body
had taken him. Himself, restless, alert
and watching now and wanting to talk

to her especially
(love, sharp, brief and briefer grown
since – in the ash of her shelled house,
curt siege I lay to her breasts, all –
yet in desire, its fumble, thunder,
lay deserts, empty, hatred, more full of)

Out of school, once more,
we've shredded and patched *the quality of mercy*.
I fold up for five minutes in the car
while wave on wave goes through my groin,
and the moment I'm through my front door,
on the phone to the surgery

(by this ghosted, ever since, have since been,
by – what I thought then – desire,
this image, her shape adrift, sweet
on the grey mirror – on earth, she, unknowing,
while feasting I was on warmth, on her,
cooling my head, its heat –

yet spawning, fast, for others, hatred –
for this was not old, lasting, old, lost, love –
nor believe it, could I bring myself –
for since – in our little deaths, nor her beaten,
marriage, we brawling, thrashing brood –
never myself, an instant, lost I sight of)

(in him neither, believe – blood-course, name,
father, could I – the clockmaker's son, caught up
in irretrievable time – nor bear talk
of bad signs of blood in shit – nights
moaning, of you at your bedside, and no-one –
where she might have been, who still

curled in the sand, dead, each day, there –
and he, voiding unbearably, his filth
into sheets and liquor only, leant help
and self-restorer – I, not useless at the last –
cursing heaven, my own wife for seeming
to love you more than the son –

and you for so stenching, crying out, *God! God!* –
paining, clock-labouring, for so
loving her, me, fleeing for His sake –
for fleeing only – for what? –
for taking me, saving me – not fighting, in hatred,
for not, years gone, dying young)

Let out of the ward on Thursday,
by Saturday the hurt's too much and he's back
in a waiting-room. I talk, try to talk
to keep his mind off the only thing
inhabiting it. He levers up,
away from the pain (thin, empty trousers

flapping, limping). Taut-mouthed
and all but incoherent under it,
to the doctor, a reel of complaints and reasons,
excuses and embarrassment
until he misses or misunderstands something,
says, *I'm sorry – sir?*

Every shred of dignity on the carpet.
Trousers down and up on the couch, to be pushed
and prodded violently, the doctor
wanting to know when it hurts.
And Dad grits his teeth, says it's okay
and means it hurts, but he can take it.

I remember it, bringing my own symptoms
coyly in, sitting at a doctor's desk,
red-handed child, ready to be quizzed
about pains and diet, exercise
and inheritance, to be prodded and pushed
and perhaps a specimen to be quite sure –

but nothing can be found.
No thing can be found – a routine blank
till he inquires whether I have anything
on my mind, particularly.
Like work and money and love and age
and my father ill?

He is only interested in the last,
noting it for posterity, saying it could be,
without minimising the case at all,
the reality of my pain, but most probably
I'm hurt in sympathy, since the mind, he says,
the imagination's a powerful thing.

(of his last putting into stranger's earth,
only bells, sunlight, a dog barking
I remember — then back, to the dark
and from bottles, no help — my brother's
clockwork curse — her fretting, cries, children
grown uncontrollable, all, all grief

but me — exiled, tradeless, careless
enough, in-wrapped enough not to need pressing —
till within a year, embarked so
for home — yet, not even home — to war on old soil,
in foreign England's name,
in my birth's country, scraped from memory —

and die there I might and paid for it too —
both, felt I, best for those I abandoned,
as I tried to do, away running
and never believed — for an instant, ever —
that, turning me, to be cleansed, enough,
say cured — enough could I have of blood)

Furnished with virtuous pills for the pain,
he starts slow on a convalescence.
He's moody, but better for the prognosis
that, on a scale of one to ten,
is not at all bad . . .
They got it. They believe. Whipped it out,

clean as a whistle. About seven and a half.
But things are not quite what they were.
He can't make use of what God gave him –
pink bags, instead, dust bags from the vacuum,
plug on his side where the stoma erupts,
red, raw, needing ointment,

the beacon of a rebellion
in the body's provinces. Weeks later,
he still leaks from the back when peeing.
He wears clown's braces, not his tightened belt,
still gets a bit giddy on the pills.
Exiled from health, but back with the living.

The knife sunk in my stomach is mine.
It's my standing in his place.
On a scale of one to ten – very likely.
What else is all this? The obsessive detail.
Acts of love of one given to silence,
wanting to speak. Tributes of a sort.

Salvation even, since I would not abandon,
could never forget, the man
I have lived for, been lived in by –
even such a voice, risen from before
the Mosque, the Synagogue, the noise
from speakers in Spitalfields' doorways –

one impossible to dissuade,
though how I can unpack such selfish hatred,
such lack of imagination,
scares me a little, though I know I ought
to love him as much as I love my father,
as I love myself, or be like him.

(enough, more than enough, and myself
not subject to it, but lucky – I mean
the shed blood, its consequences, in which,
I dreamed – out of it now – shadows once more,
of her – across the cold floor, blood-warm
beside me, back turned, her breasts,

my hand between them, as a book,
my finger in it, that I cannot lay aside –
and for this, not knowing
she will have me back, or whether no –
yet in hope – to others and beyond others,
turn my attention – so spent, have I,

this sum of last weeks – my slow trudge,
returning out of blood – at construing people,
the living, dead of London, dunes of France –
even the yet to live, inheritors yet –
all these must I learn to love – or exile
myself, or bear the future refugee)

POST

Yellow Pages

Here are three new lives begun,
though we don't know it yet
as we push open the door,
its sudden kick-start
into a spluttering, uneven life

with a full Moses basket
precarious on the coffee table,
my hands suddenly empty
and full of responsibility
and the flappy, panicky,
What the hell do we do now?

because he's suddenly crying
(and the toilet doesn't flush)
and the health visitor at the door
can only stay a moment

and I remember, right there,
in the small of my back,
his rigid forearm as I swayed
above the spokes, his hand
on the saddle, those same
dry knuckles on my hands now

scarred and survived
and something to settle me
for what the push, once begun,
has not the power to recall

and the eventual stranger
drops his tool-bag in our porch,
lifts his hand to the door.

Lips

As I lie down beside him,
the sofa-world he must think of
as wholly his own, flexes
to one side and he stares up
at my raised arm, overarching

a stubby fingerprinted tree

the other bringing its hand
to the both of us, bringing
a digestive biscuit
to visit my mouth
while he watches rapt, blue, wide,
swinging into each mouthful

so eloquent, so without words,
my crumb-speckled lips
going about their business.

A documentary

Adrift now, under the river-storm
that comes down with every day,
I can find no glimpse
of the other side – the place
of the orderly, the sweet rhyme

since these past few weeks
of days, the child, night feeds,
are the knuckled heads
of alligators in the river-flood
that gives television, one evening

repeating a documentary
on the strange zealous sect
who live on cremation grounds
off excreta and burnt flesh,
acting out what they know

– the more of such pollution,
the less they need rub their eyes
for what matters, what survives.

Footprint

There is shock in such a vacancy,
the way quiet has hit this house,
though this is how it used to be
a matter of weeks ago,
when we would sit to imagine
and neither managed the truth of this

– my prowling the length and breadth
of rooms without sense,
without rest, unable to hold
to anything, a marooned Crusoe,
gaze lifting to pick the horizon,
eyes dawdling to the street
for nothing, for a first sight
of rescue, the snap of feet
gone to walk in Stationers' Park

till I dawdle to a stop
at his last night's bed, cot sheets
not yet changed, his shape
no more than a footprint
pressed into the sand, spelling
the familiar twist in the tale.

A try-out

You were almost silence enough
to last both our lifetimes,
near substantive absence,
sky-big and earth-secure,
the guilt like a huddled child
in every corner of us

– almost the prickle of darkness
pinned about us as parents,
inescapable at noon,
oppressive in the night
when it would fall upon us,
as we lay with the knowledge
you'd grown still, grown
small enough to creep
to the heart's core and kill

and keep us alive
as we thought to cancel you,
yet would never have been free,
become something beside which
we'd measure our lives

almost not even a memory,
a try-out, a false-trail,
our best chance, known best work
now, not being ourselves,
but astonished and complete.

Nightmare

His first, its sudden grotesque
smashing up
through the trusted surface
of sleep, a scrabbling clutch
to be escaped from,
a tightening on leg and arm,
fastened to his vulnerable
heart, stomach, breath

– yet what manner of thing
is it makes him burst
into real tears,
the bewildering touch of night,
inconsolable, though stroked
and held to, brought
to familiar light, our warmth

what nightmare, monstrous,
risen black-combed and dripping
from sleep must it be

– and the question enough
to rattle his father too,
as if such innocence and trust,
such never-known-hurt, nor
arm-raised, voice-raised, neglect
or loneliness
could find such ground for fear,
then could not he, or one
with hardly more reason

invent evil and ride
the monster back to the deep
and back still further to waking?

La-la-la

In the thickest of night,
before the altar of this crying
god, I kneel down

my head swollen with the hours
through which I have not moved,
thinking only, if only
I could propitiate
with a touch, with a *la-la-la*,
persuade my unsettled darling
to withdraw a while from the world

then I'd follow, his greatest
enthusiast, as I am
all day long, when his few pounds
belly-out a springy canvas chair
and I play music
thumping with rhythm and noise

and dance for his delight

for those waving arms
that I'm certain make answer
to my own, my stamp-stamp
and shake about the heart,
my hands up, hooray,
as spirits fly through the air,
infantile and optimistic

and too quickly gone,
especially now, kneeling here
in the dark – he turns, bursts.

The gift

I watch my son catch at grace
each day, his every beginning
to make sense
a glimpse of rhyme

like the series of quiet-breathing
shapes like balloons
that bob into sight, opening
black with noise,
with *la-la-la* – a likeness,
a kind of confidence there
that can be worked up

as between the grasping shapes,
wrigglers he can have rise
on either side of himself
to make a match with those more
monstrous ones that descend
and turn him, lift and stroke

– a similitude, suddenly,
that will go on inviting
until he grows too familiar,
for ten, a dozen years,
so little time, then find
whatever art renews the gift
that lay open to him

a knowledge unlike knowledge

the gut-hope and heart-felt smile
of a companionable world.

Loneliness

The more he knows of himself,
the more he knows of the dark
and not just of night,
but absence as well

– my walking out of the room
to answer the phone, the door,
to fix up his food

and his way then, is arms akimbo,
aware enough to know well
the light's shorn from the world,
yet not enough aware
to believe that it will return

so arms wide and a great cry
from the endless Sahara
he's left looking into
with absolute certainty

the cat's scent of the well

that uncluttered nature.

Recognition

You are the crystal for which
this supersaturation
of word and rhythm has waited

my great yes at last, active mood,
imperative, call to arms,
welcome orders to tread lines
like these with the ebb and flow
that comes naturally to me

that go pushing
down the ways of innocence
(and every one is your way now)
though drawn to an incline
long since mapped out, where you'll
plunge headlong for knowledge,
for chance and change,
for lives not taken, not renewed

and each several declension
from the scrupulous true
is one more aspect of that
complex of faces I write out now
and recognise as you.

Skin

I roll awake three hours
before dawn into his unconscious
scuffing – how even
in sleep he must fight it

this thing that must seem evil
as hunger and cold
do not since they can be cured,
since even I can cure them
by holding, simple, attendant
till we have both grown content

– yet this sly blanketing by fire,
this pricking body's mask,
this glove-fit visitor, especially
in the night, is too craven
to prosecute open war,
so lures with promise of relief
and breeds at a touch

till now I lie quite awake,
listen to his rest invaded,
his worrying at it like memory,
like hurt, like years to come.

A tiny prison

Little one, you look to me
for the best use of words

but scour a life-time of them
and I'd be wrong to believe
they do not fall short
of the hurt, the helplessness
at seeing you reel,
enveloped in your other self,
your needling, unrelenting skin
that turns you from new desire
to a tiny prison

– as when you reach for my face,
jerked back, a puppet's hand,
to your own cheeks
and grown more busy there
to call a livid madder ghost

and I'd be wrong to say
(though I try to put this right)
that with each retraction,
with each snap of the string

you do not dwindle from me.

Something we did

One single passer-by's burst
of *Oh, Jesus!* as she's looking
at the look of your face,
sinks us both low all night,
most of the next morning,
falling in with her vicious
and unspoken accusation

that we are to blame
in lacking the curative touch
of good parents, their effortless
virtues elbowed aside
by our illogical, untrue,
more than suspicion that will not
take no, that she may be right

– it's this that withers
our hearts to these dry husks
for something we did,
for something we've never done

and so to blame, even now
not knowing how to help clear
your cheek's raw crust,
the marbled, bloody scratch-pan
of chin that you have, harrowed
darling, O Jesus, your face.

New lullaby

With a mournful recital
he has sung himself to sleep
and we lay him in the dark
only to sail out once in a while,
transmitted to a second room

a sigh and hush-hush
of bedclothes that to us
is some fabulous beast
stirred towards a dream

till a glimpse of back,
rolling half above, below waves,
then risen, dripping,
with the deep still upon him,
a squealing that wants a touch,
a voice, intuitive,
calming some colt or dog
or little bird and fainting back

into the old whale song
ground out, tidal, original,
slurred and drawing up
every ounce of unsleep out of limbs,
gathered slowly to a point
and let go as he slips

shy yet to come to our hands.

Head tale

We carry your brief story
from waiting-room to consultation,
from ward to radiologist,
repeating ourselves, our prayer,
blessing, curse, conjuring
of spirits, we do not know
which, have no grasp
of anything except the detail

as incontrovertibly yours
as the shape of your eyes,
still recognisably
the almond scowl that broke me up
under puffed, birth-purple brows

as much yours as the misshapen
boulder, your head, the reason
we're here, fearing the past
like a monster stirring
some old thread of the tale

and this promenade of white coats
seems to work from the same list
of possibilities,
so each time they delete
one more horror, your story grows
longer till, thank christ,
at last, this list of months
and symptoms, fears and diagnoses,
this ordinary unique
that amounts to the little
you've had of life and feels to us
already like everything

to the noters and nodders,
the listeners to what we say,
it signifies now nothing, normal.

Restless child

(Bolingbroke Castle)

There was nothing much here
to speak of, then something
fallen quickly to dereliction
till an antiquarian
recovered what we stop for

– grassy hummocks of the great hall,
the kitchen tower,
the auditor's tower,
food and money amounting to power
that died back into itself

and this for us
is how the world is engineered
like poetry's
eventual snap of rhyme
(after the long accumulation)
that too soon grows familiar,
dulled and forgotten
till we are slapped awake

perhaps, to ditched pasture
like this, that's buttered today
with the most brilliant sunshine,
the flock at rest, the business
of barons, the behind-doors,
far off, once present, gone

and my minutes cut short
by a restless child who takes me
all but empty-handed,
or hands full of straws and one
is wanting to write something
with this beauty in it.

Empty the bath

Late and quiet with all my keys
for the door, I hope you've not
yet been laid in your cot,
but find in the bathroom
a tubful of water, empty, well-
used and barely lukewarm

and to tell you the truth,
there's the earth of my regret,
the little warmth the water has,
its tiny fractions
stolen from your playful heat

how it shows I've come too late
for the intimacy
of your straight-backed body
cut at the waist by cooling water,
those few gallons of sudsy wash
that cooled that much more slowly
for you being there

that now I let go, stir away
with both hands, think something
obvious, grasping what is gone.

The short light

You must feel the new season
in the new angle of light,
its sheer, longer visits
bringing fresh threads of air
that no longer come raw
to your livid cheeks

and there's a touch of green
in the hedge by the door
where there were only grey twigs,
unmistakable, even to eyes
as ill-tuned as yours and yet
(you will not know this)
it has come early this year,
this walking through flowers,
these crocuses under trees

nor have you seen how the years
will turn upon themselves,
devour their tails

so you might have imagined
this amelioration
of light and air, of earth
and us, marks such a change
in the core of your short light,
that it cannot ever wither,
be withdrawn in its turn,
will go on being given like love.

You wave

All three of us are there
for the forge moment, the sweet
rhyme and rent veil
of your morning uncovering

as you squat between our nakedness
in cheery hoops,
touch the hair on my head
and unprompted find your way

to the darker, tighter curls
from which you withdrew
one half of yourself, then reach
for the sketchiest of lines
you ruffle on my chest
with almost a dash these days

with an independent hand

with something close to words,
though you cannot speak them,
their shapes clear in mind,
in crossing our tongues
and brought with gestures
to a world that will respond,
our equivocal delight
as you wave *window*, then *door*.

Hold me

Your word for the birds
that swing perky on the nuts
is exactly the same
as for the light as it burns
in its paper lantern

the same clear sound
you use for tiger, rag doll,
a photo of two cousins,
Andrew and Christopher

not unlike the one
you use for 'hungry', 'dirty',
'hold me, hold me'

– first stab at the eloquence
you will fall away from
to be precise.

Kyrie

(The Maltings, Snape)

A solitary candle, tomorrow,
will seem light enough
for you to pick your own way
through the night's invitation
into the second of your summers

so tonight, while we drive,
A year ago – a year ago today,
we waited, packed and ready,
drinks, nightdress, radio, books
we talk and we see

as in some fairground mirror,
slips and swathes, sudden
glimpses of ourselves in you
that show we had no control,
the sweet deal in the dark
was a first and last shuffling
of utterly simple gifts

– and to mark the year's eve,
we leave you with grandparents,
set aside for ourselves
this great breadth of blue sky,
this echo of our humility
and the faithlessness of things
is in the fen-wind's blessing,
blow and blessing, then blow
where we hear it beyond the walls,
under the tenor's Latin verse

his *Carry me, Carry me*

as we hear it now, driving home,
each listening, leant right in
for a breath in the baby-dark.

Other books in the same series include

ANNA ADAMS *Green Resistance: New and Selected Poems*

SEBASTIAN BARKER *The Hand in the Well*

FRANCES CORNFORD *Selected Poems*

KEVIN CROSSLEY-HOLLAND *The Language of Yes*

KEVIN CROSSLEY-HOLLAND *Poems from East Anglia*

HILARY DAVIES *In a Valley of This Restless Mind*

DAVID GASCOYNE *Selected Prose*

DAVID GASCOYNE *Selected Verse Translations*

PHOEBE HESKETH *A Box of Silver Birch*

JEREMY HOOKER *Our Lady of Europe*

JUDITH KAZANTZIS *Swimming Through the Grand Hotel*

BLAKE MORRISON & PAULA REGO *Pendle Witches*

VICTOR PASMORE *The Man Within*

RUTH PITTER *Collected Poems*

JEREMY REED *Sweet Sister Lyric*

ANTHONY THWAITE *Selected Poems 1956-1996*

EDWARD UPWARD *Christopher Isherwood: Notes in Remembrance of a Friendship*

EDWARD UPWARD *The Scenic Railway*